WORLD'S GREATEST ATHLETES

Landon DONOVAN

By James Buckley, Jr.

The Child's World
www.childsworld.com

Published in the United States of America by The Child's World®
P.O. Box 326 • Chanhassen, MN 55317-0326
800-599-READ • www.childsworld.com

ACKNOWLEDGMENTS

The Child's World®: Mary Berendes, Publishing Director

Produced by Shoreline Publishing Group LLC
President / Editorial Director: James Buckley, Jr.
Designer: Tom Carling, carlingdesign.com
Assistant Editor: Ellen Labrecque

Photo Credits
Cover: AP/Wide World
Interior: AP/Wide World: 24, 26; Corbis: 7; Getty Images: 3, 5, 8, 10, 12, 15, 18, 21, 25, 28; WireImage: 1, 16

LIBRARY OF CONGRESS
CATALOGING-IN-PUBLICATION DATA

Buckley, James, 1963–
  Landon Donovan / by James Buckley, Jr.
      p. cm. — (The world's greatest athletes)
  Includes bibliographical references and index.
  ISBN 1-59296-754-X (library bound : alk. paper)
  1. Donovan, Landon, 1982——Juvenile literature. 2. Soccer players—
United States—Biography—Juvenile literature. I. Title. II. Series.
  GV942.7.D66B83 2006
  796.334092—dc22

                                    2006006283

CONTENTS

INTRODUCTION
America's Best Soccer Player 4

CHAPTER 1
From AYSO to Life as a Pro 6

CHAPTER 2
To Germany—And Then Home 12

CHAPTER 3
Donovan Still Dominates 20

CAREER STATISTICS 29
GLOSSARY 30
FIND OUT MORE 31
INDEX AND ABOUT THE AUTHOR 32

America's Best Soccer Player

NOT TOO LONG AGO, BEING THE BEST SOCCER player in America was sort of like being the best baseball player in England. Only a few people knew about you, and even fewer cared. Soccer was a sport that many kids played, but few people followed on the pro level. The sport, however, has enjoyed explosive growth in the United States since the mid-1990s. Since 1995, Major League Soccer (MLS), a 12-team pro league, has grown steadily in popularity. The U.S. national team has earned spots in the last five World Cups, the **international** championship held every four years. U.S. players have earned notice with their play on the best pro teams in Europe.

As the sport has grown, top U.S. players have gotten more attention. Now, being the best soccer player in America is something millions of young players across the country are shooting for.

The player most experts feel holds that title now is Landon Donovan, a young, high-scoring striker from California. Not too long ago, Landon was just another one of the kids racing around a suburban field. In just a few years, he has become one of the top goal-scorers in the world.

His amazing rise from little kid in big shorts to international superstar has been the result of not only his great talent, but a nose for the goal rare in an American player. As the U.S. has improved its play, scoring goals has not been its best skill. Landon is changing that, for his (Major League Soccer) MLS team and the national squad. The best player in America won't be a mystery much longer.

Donovan has appeared in more than 75 games for the U.S. national team.

CHAPTER 1

From AYSO to Life as a Pro

LANDON WAS BORN IN 1982 AND IT SEEMED AS if he was kicking a soccer ball before he got out of diapers. Landon got his start on a real soccer field at the age of five in Redlands, California, east of Los Angeles. He joined a team of six- and seven-year-olds and scored seven goals in his first game. He played on youth league teams and soon joined the ranks of "club" soccer. This level of play is much higher than American Youth Soccer Organization (AYSO—a large national youth league). Club players practice more often and travel to play in tournaments. Most top players have spent a lot of time in the club programs.

Landon's club was Cal Heat, and he was a top goal-scorer for them. Early on, he displayed his abilities to keep the ball on his feet in a crowd of

A future Landon Donovan? Landon was about these young players' age when he started scoring goals for his team.

players, and his skill at being near the goal at the right time. In 1997, he caught the attention of the Olympic Development Program (ODP), a group that searches for America's top young players. The ODP took Landon another big step up the ladder toward his dream of a pro career. He went to a camp in Montana to train with other top young players.

At the same time, he was also taking part in high school soccer, first for Redlands High and then

The latest U.S. star to emerge from the U-17 teams is teenager Freddy Adu, here playing against Sierra Leone.

as a top scorer for nearby East Valley High. His work with the ODP kept him away at times, but he still managed to score 16 goals in 10 games for East Valley. In his second year with them, he scored 15 goals and racked up 19 assists. After that season, he was named to *Parade* magazine's All-America team.

A large number of international soccer tournaments are held at the age-group level. In 1998,

Donovan joined the U.S. Under-16 team and took part in games matching the United States against other nations. He scored three goals in a tournament final against South Korea, part of his total of 23 goals that year for the U-16s, as teams like that are known.

With each stop on his rocket-like soccer ride, Landon kept scoring and improving. Next up was a new training program called Project 2010, designed to find and train the best young soccer players in the country, with a goal of World Cup success by the year 2010. Landon spent time at a special school in Florida set up for this team, taking regular school classes, but also training hard every day.

Now a year older, he was part of the U-17 team that scored one of America's top soccer victories ever, a 4–3 win in 1999 against powerful Argentina. Naturally, Landon scored two goals in the game. Later that year, he was called all the way up for an appearance with the U-23 team, making him, at 17, the youngest U.S. player ever at that level, which is just one away from the top national squad.

Landon could see his goal of a pro career in sight. He knew he was among the best, and he remained there even as he played on better and better teams.

The United States has men's soccer teams at the U-14, U-16, U-17, U-19, and U-23 levels. America's future World Cup stars are trained on these teams.

"I knew I had a shot at an international career when I was going through the development programs," he said in 2000. "I made a state team, went to some camps, and saw what it was like. I realized when I was about 15 that if I kept going like I was, I would make it [to the pro level]."

Playing against the top young players from around the world for these various age-group teams, Landon was also catching the eye of top international

This tackle is typical of how the young forward was treated in the rough-and-tumble world of German pro soccer.

Young Landon Donovan

- Was league MVP twice in high school

- Took violin lessons in grade school

- In first-ever appearance in international soccer, scored a goal for the U.S. U-17 team against Mexico

- Signed big contract to promote Nike at the same time he signed with German pro club

teams. In most other countries, especially in Europe, soccer teams are bigger than NFL or Major League Baseball teams are in the United States. The biggest soccer clubs search the world for the best players, and pay big money to lure talent to their teams. A number of these clubs asked Landon to try out.

In 1999, Landon's dream finally came true. He signed a professional contract with Bayer Leverkusen, a team near Dusseldorf, Germany. The little kid who scored seven goals in his first game had become a much-sought-after star, heading far from home to chase goals on and off the soccer field.

Making new dreams come true turned out to be more difficult than he thought.

CHAPTER 2

To Germany— And Then Home

GERMANY WAS A LONG WAY FROM SOUTHERN California, and from Landon's family, and Landon didn't speak a word of German. Still only 17 years old, Landon found the adjustment to European life hard. The soccer was harder, too. He was not put on the Bayer first team right away, but played with its lower-level teams. In the spring of 1999, he spent all his time with his new German club, but he also continued to have a job to do with several U.S. national teams. The split of his time would prove to be a problem for his German bosses.

In the summer, he helped the U.S. place third at the Pan Am Games, an international sports event like the Olympics, but only for countries from North and South America and the Caribbean.

Next up for Landon was the U-17 World Championships. This U-17 team was among the best America had ever produced. They had not lost in the 20 **matches** leading up to the tournament, and Landon himself had scored 32 goals in 35 games. In the opening matches, Landon scored goals in a win over New Zealand and a tie against Poland. Unfortunately, in the tournament semifinals, even a goal by Landon could not knock off Australia. The U.S. lost after a penalty-kick shootout. Even though the U.S. finished fourth, Landon won the Golden Ball as the most valuable player of the tournament.

Another big event for Landon in 2000 was the Summer Olympics. National U-23 teams represent their countries at the Olympics. Though still only 18, Landon was named to the squad. However, in the first few games before and during the Olympic tournament, Landon was frustrated when coaches often kept him on the bench in favor of older players. He was itching to get in and show what he could do on one of the biggest international sports stages.

At the Games, he didn't get his chance until the third match, against Kuwait. His late goal clinched a 3–1 victory, and America moved past the first round for the first time in Olympic soccer history. Though their medal hopes ended with a loss to Spain, the U.S. squad had played well.

Meanwhile, Landon remained signed to a pro contract with Bayer Leverkusen. Between all his

Who's the blond? That's Landon, who dyed his hair blond during the 2000 Summer Olympics.

As the top scorer for every team he's been on, Donovan is often a marked man and often finds himself on the ground.

trips with U.S. national teams—not unusual in pro soccer, but still a hassle for coaches—Landon had not been able to practice with the Germans as much as his coaches wanted. They kept him on the bench or playing with lower-division teams. Landon's experience in Germany was turning out to be negative. He was not getting the playing time he wanted. Regular play for a pro club was what he needed to improve his game.

Though playing in Europe was, and for many players still is, the **ultimate** goal, Landon had to make a tough choice. Working with his agent, Bayer officials, and MLS leaders, America's top young scoring threat worked out a deal to come home. Officially, he was still signed with Bayer, but they agreed to "loan" him to MLS. Still not even 19 years old, Landon joined the San Jose Earthquakes of MLS.

In 2005, he told fans, "[Not fitting into the German league] wasn't a matter of personality. The players and coaching staff were very nice to me. It simply became a matter of not playing, and for whatever reason, I wasn't playing. That made my decision [to come home] easy."

For their part, the Earthquakes were excited.

"Once we knew there was a chance to get him, we were thrilled," San Jose coach Frank Yallop said at the time. "Although he's a young man, he's proved that he's a very good player. He's going to be a bright star of the future."

For San Jose, the future came right away. In his first start, Landon scored a goal against the MetroStars; by midseason, the formerly unsuccessful Earthquakes led the Western Division. Landon was

In His Own Words

Landon spent nearly two years in Germany. In Internet chats with fans, he reflected on what he learned there:

▶ *"It was a very humbling experience to come from high school and the U-17 team to working with so many great players in Germany. I learned a lot, especially how to deal with tough situations. I also learned to value my family and friends more.*

▶ *"The best part about playing was probably the atmosphere and attention surrounding the game. Every game was a huge production, no matter who we were playing.*

▶ *"I learned many interesting things about the German culture, and I also learned that the way they live their lives imitates the way they play soccer. I find that to be true with most countries around the world, interestingly enough."*

a huge fan favorite and was named a starter on the midseason All-Star team. The All-Star game was held in San Jose, and Landon put on a show for the home folks, scoring a record four goals. He was named the MVP. It was good to have the nation's top scorer back on home turf.

The successes just kept coming for Landon and the 'Quakes, as they won the division title and advanced to the playoffs. This was a huge jump for a team that had won only 7 of 32 games the previous season. Led by Landon, San Jose made the championship game, the MLS Cup, for the first time. Trailing 1–0 to the Los Angeles Galaxy, the 'Quakes turned to their newest star. He hammered home the tying goal in the first half. The exciting game went to sudden-death overtime, and when Dwayne DeRosario headed home a goal, Landon was a champion for the first time in his pro career.

The decision to come home looked like it had been a good one. Next up for Landon was an even bigger job: leading the U.S. team to the biggest stage in soccer—the World Cup.

Donovan Still Dominates

THE BIG 2002 EVENT FOR EVERY SOCCER FAN IN the world—and, of course, for Landon—was the World Cup. Held every four years, it matches the best players from the best soccer nations. The 2002 event was held in South Korea and Japan; 32 teams, including the U.S., made the finals. The teams were divided into eight groups of four teams each. In the U.S. group were powerful Portugal, home favorite South Korea, and Poland. It didn't look good for Landon and his teammates. But that's why they play the games on the field, not on paper, as the old saying goes.

Against Portugal, the U.S. scored twice early on and suddenly a game they were supposed to lose became one they could win. They went up 3–0, but

A victory by Donovan and the U.S. team over Portugal in 2002 put the American team on the world soccer map.

Portugal, led by international star Luís Figo, fought back to score twice. Still, the U.S. held on and earned a hard-fought and surprising victory.

Next up was Korea, playing in front of a huge, roaring pro-Korea crowd. The U.S. seemed to be **affected** by their surroundings and they looked

It looks the goalie might get it, but he didn't! Landon secured the U.S. World Cup match victory over Mexico in 2002.

out of sorts. They gave up a penalty kick early, but goalie Brad Friedel made a great save on a shot that normally goes in. The U.S scored to take the lead, but Korea tied it. The game ended 1–1. Now a victory over Poland would send the U.S. into the second round. Unfortunately, the U.S. lost to the Poles 3–1. Thanks to a big win by Korea over Portugal, however, the U.S. squeaked into the next round and a match against archrival Mexico.

In one of the biggest games in U.S. soccer history, the U.S. won, 2–0. Landon's goal (see box on page 24) sealed the victory. Even though the U.S. lost to eventual runner-up Germany in the next game, the 2002 World Cup was the most successful in U.S. soccer history.

After the excitement of the World Cup, it was back to MLS business for Landon. He picked up right where he had left off, leading the Earthquakes to another MLS Cup championship in 2003. He scored a sudden-death overtime goal in the semifinals and then scored twice in the final game. He was named the MLS Cup MVP and also earned his first U.S. Soccer Player of the Year award.

In 2004, Landon and MLS fans got a shock when

Landon's Big Moment

For many years, Mexico has been the United States' biggest rival in soccer. Not only are they our closest neighbor to the south, the sport is enormously popular there. When the national team plays, businesses sometimes stop work and schools close so that people can watch the games.

Mexico usually wins against the United States. In fact, they once won every game between the two nations for more than 40 years. Though the U.S. had beaten Mexico in 2001, Mexico was favored when the two teams met in the round of 16 at the 2002 World Cup. During that game, Landon scored perhaps his most important goal.

The U.S. had taken a 1-0 lead early on a goal by Brian McBride. Mexico threatened time and again, but could not score. The U.S. defense was tiring under the pressure. With less than 30 minutes to go, Landon rose above a crowd of players to head in a goal! The 2-0 cushion allowed the U.S. to control the game. They held on to win and post the biggest victory in U.S. soccer history since the U.S. defeated England in another World Cup game . . . in 1950!

Bayer Leverkusen (remember that Landon was just on "loan" to MLS) asked him to come back to Germany. However, another deal was worked out and Landon was instead traded to the Los Angeles Galaxy, another MLS team.

Landon's journey through soccer had taken him from near Los Angeles, around the world to play in tournaments, to Germany to play as a pro (and to play there again for the U.S. during the 2006 World Cup), and to San Jose to become a champion. Now, with the Galaxy, he was finally, really home.

"You have no idea how good it is to be back home and able to play in Southern California," he said after joining the Galaxy. "My time in San Jose was fantastic and I wouldn't trade it for anything. But now I love the team and the situation I'm in now."

During his first season with Galaxy in 2005, Landon was also helping the U.S. team qualify

Donovan assists his teammates with perfect passing form.

Thanks in part to Landon's goal-scoring and playmaking abilities, the Los Angeles Galaxy hoisted the MLS Cup in 2005.

for its fifth World Cup in a row, held in Germany in the summer of 2006. He tied Eddie Johnson for the national team lead with seven goals, and also had the most assists with eight.

He was also a key part of the Galaxy's drive toward the 2005 MLS playoffs, scoring 12 goals on the season. For the third time, he helped an MLS team reach the MLS Cup, this time leading the Galaxy into a battle with the New England Revolution.

A tough New England defense kept Landon bottled up for most of the game, and neither team scored after the 90-minute regular time. In sudden-death, the Galaxy's Carlos Ruiz scored and L.A. was the champ. Landon had won his third MLS Cup!

In just six years as a pro soccer player, Landon has twice led his nation to a spot in the World Cup, three times led his MLS team to a league championship, and won three national player of the year awards. Imagine what this great young soccer star will do as he gets older—and better!

Looking to the future, as he always does, Landon has a message for young players. "I am almost overwhelmed by the quantity of good, young

American players right now. Even better than that, there are hundreds of 12-, 13-, 14-year-olds who will probably be better than we are now."

America's best soccer player seems to be saying that America's next best soccer player might be holding this book right now.

See you in the World Cup!

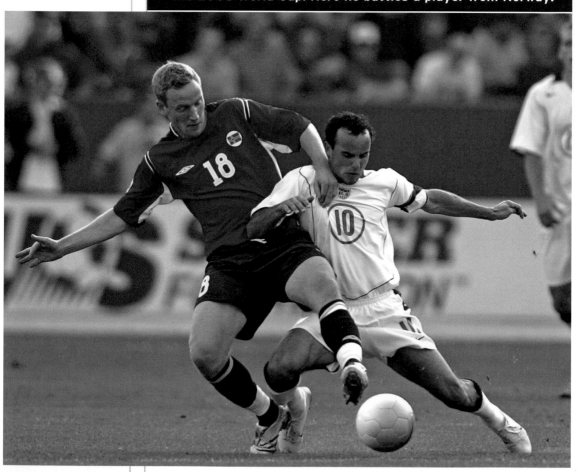

Landon's latest success was helping the U.S. earn a spot in the 2006 World Cup. Here he battles a player from Norway.

Landon Donovan's Career Statistics

MLS

Year	Team	Games	Goals	Assists
2001	San Jose	22	7	10
2002	San Jose	20	7	3
2003	San Jose	22	12	6
2004	San Jose	23	6	10
2005	Los Angeles	22	12	1
Career		109	44	39

U.S. NATIONAL TEAM

	GP/GS	MIN	G	A	Pts
2000	1/0	58	1	1	3
2001	8/7	634	0	0	0
2002	20/17	1563	6	0	12
2003	15/13	1224	7	5	19
2004	14/14	1243	5	5	15
2005	15/12	1169	6	6	18
2006	4/4	360	0	2	2
Totals	77/67	6251	25	22	

Legend: GP/GS: games played, games started; **MIN**: Minutes played; **G**: goals; **A**: assists; **Pts**: points (goals are counted as two points in stats, though only one in games; an assist earns a player one statistical point, but none in games)

as of May 10, 2006

GLOSSARY

affected bothered by, influenced by

atmosphere in this case, the surroundings of a big soccer game—the crowd, the noise, the stadium, the pressure

imitates copies, does the same as

international in the case of soccer, games and tournaments played between the national teams of different countries

match word used in soccer for a single game

ultimate the best, the last

BOOKS

The Everything Kids' Soccer Book: Rules, Techniques, and More about Your Favorite Sport!
By Deborah W. Crisfield
(Adams Media Corporation, Massachusetts) 2003
This book contains tips on how to improve your play, plus facts on soccer stars, including Landon Donovan and women's star Mia Hamm.

Landon Donovan: World Class Soccer Star
By Rebecca Thatcher Murcia
(Mitchell Lane Publishers, Delaware) 2005
This book follows Donovan's career playing for the national team, Major League Soccer, and in Europe. Includes many full-color action photographs.

Thanks to Donovan, MLS's Cup could runneth over
By Scott Plagenhoef
Soccer Digest, January 1, 2002 issue
Volume 24, Issue 5
This article focuses on Donovan's influence on Major League Soccer after leading the San Jose Earthquakes to the 2001 MLS Cup.

Time Is on Their Side
By Scott Plagenhoef
Soccer Digest, June 1, 2001 issue
Volume 24, Issue 2
This article states that Landon Donovan, Bobby Convey, and DaMarcus Beasley are among the next generation of U.S. soccer stars who hope to win a World Cup.

WEB SITES

Visit our home page for lots of links about Landon Donovan: www.childsworld.com/links

Note to Parents, Teachers, and Librarians: We routinely check our Web links to make sure they're safe, active sites—so encourage your readers to check them out!

INDEX

Adu, Freddy, 8
All-America team, 8
All-Star team, 19
American Youth Soccer Organization (AYSO), 6

Bayer Leverkusen and Germany, 10, 11, 13, 15–17, 18, 25

Cal Heat, 6–7
career statistics, 29
childhood, 5, 6–7
club soccer, 6

DeRosario, Dwayne, 19

endorsement deals, 11

Figo, Luís, 22
Friedel, Brad, 23

goal-scoring skills, 5, 6, 16, 19, 26, 27
Golden Ball, 14

high school soccer, 7–8

Johnson, Eddie, 27

Los Angeles Galaxy, 19, 25–27

Major League Soccer (MLS), 4, 17, 23, 25
McBride, Brian, 24
message for young players, 27–28

MLS Cup of 2001, 19
MLS Cup of 2003, 23
MLS Cup of 2005, 26, 27
Most Valuable Player (MVP), 11, 19, 23

Nike deal, 11

Olympic Development Program (ODP), 7, 8

Pan Am Games, 13
professional status, 10, 11, 13, 15
Project 2010, 9

record breaking, 11, 19
Ruiz, Carlos, 27

San Jose Earthquakes, 17, 19, 23
soccer camp, 7, 10
soccer in Europe, 10, 11
soccer in Mexico, 24
soccer in the U.S., 4
Summer Olympics of 2000, 14–15

Under-16 national team, 9
Under-17 national team, 8, 11, 14, 18
Under-23 national team, 9, 14
U.S. Soccer Player of the Year, 23, 27

Western Division, 17, 19
World Cup of 1950, 24
World Cup of 2002, 20–23, 24
World Cup of 2006, 25, 27, 28
World Cup of 2010, 9

ABOUT THE AUTHOR

James Buckley, Jr. has written more than 40 books on sports and other topics for young readers. Along with books on soccer, which he has played since he was seven years old (though not as well as Landon Donovan, of course!), he has written about baseball, football, NASCAR, and the Olympics. He lives in Santa Barbara, California.